Some Cares

Benjamin Friedlander

SPUYTEN DUYVIL

New York City

"Dimension," "Cognition Is Its Own Discard," and "Funeral" were previously published in *The Brooklyn Rail*. The author thanks Anselm Berrigan for their inclusion.

Library of Congress Control Number: 2023951998

                    like snow
upon some Tuesday afternoon in winter
coming to ground to be held a little while
then melt to whispered coagulating rain

—Marsden Hartley

SOME CARES

DIMENSION

Stretching a point
into a line,

the seed cannot divulge
its cause, only result:

it makes a mystery of that creation
to which it draws our attention.

How does a model
amplify a method?

A method, its concept?
~~Like pulling a door open~~

~~against wind.~~ Like points
becoming a line, or lines a plane;

planes, a solid:
things grow

most surprisingly
in participation.

All form is organic, even time
is creaturely. Active connections

reinforced
by experience

stabilize, while weak ones disappear.
In observance of the light

the night is closed
for maintenance

Atmospheric
conditions:

permeated
by sun

smearing color
everywhere.

The depth is not great
but ~~lungs will collapse~~

~~reaching it~~ an axle
will snap

getting across ~~The piles~~
~~of snow~~

~~sink into themselves~~
the dip

Complex Fault-Tolerant System

A balloon
needn't be popped:

its tautness will soften
and gravity do the rest.

~~When we come to the end of our natural days,~~
~~our natural night is the only way forward.~~

Nothing is beyond

imagination:

all that might be

succumbs to thought—

if not now, then someday. Flags
wrapped around a pole

show wind was here,
now gone.

Lilacs in bloom—
their purple tips reach high,

I see them
from my bed.

Here
where thought

is what wilts,
shrinking

from light, resolution
comes from below.

All that pertains isn't useful glitters gold

Grim hymnody

whispered through a decade

Every sentence
an act of trespass.

I provide salted plums,
do not return to harmony and beauty.

Spurned in the gesture
of embrace, the welcome

of the western horizon
to the sun

sends day on its way
without emotion.

WHISPERS

The sandpaper of language
brushed against time.[1]

[1] **It Hurts**

I don't know which
is more exquisite: the blue

of this evening sky,
or the realization it withholds.

Silence redeems the noise

redeems the silence
holding nothing back.
Shadows scratch the sun

down
dragging
confidence

out of sight. The walls recede,
the room
gets huge ~~unseeable~~

~~in the dark~~
~~swallowing pride~~
~~spitting me out~~

Kept awake by an itch
I couldn't reach,
I scratched what I could, which wasn't me.

~~Itching is a tingling~~
~~or irritation~~
~~of the skin~~

~~that makes you want to score~~
~~the affected area with a sharp~~
~~or pointed~~

~~object, sometimes leading to infection. Nails~~
~~against a blackboard~~ This
is its very
definition: to stir up,

provoke,
give rise
to an action,

a feeling;
~~A scab I don't recall~~
~~catches me~~
~~as I rub~~
~~my leg~~
~~with my leg~~
~~under covers~~ Good night, says the moon,
looking away,

trailing silver The quiet
sky
purples ~~Tactility is in the hand of its beholder~~
~~Listening is an intimate act~~

WATER IS LIQUID, ICE IS SOLID, WHAT IS SNOW? YAHOO ANSWERS

a line
of credit widened
by malice
into a smile

self-inflicted, hereditary, a public stigma
of a degenerate and corrupt ancestry
It is thought to be without remedy
in purgatory or redemption in eternity

Snow is congealed Vapour. Hail is congealed Rain

held in tension

Matter in the form of a steamy or imperceptible ex-
halation

Untried pleasures deadened into styles

convert, rescind ~~reasoning~~
~~cuts through a multitude of sensations~~

~~My paywall, peripheral~~
~~& symbolic, is~~

~~no more, forever,~~

~~a making-~~
~~free~~
~~enterprise~~
I'm done

One last puzzle
  to unpiece and throw
    into the box

Where people pass, but never on foot, money is strip-
mined from cities.

COGNITION IS ITS OWN DISCARD

Putting its weight
into action, into motion, first the days fade out,

then memory,
then memory's prompts,

then we disappear
into the same fog.[‡]

> [‡] ~~Check~~

> ~~Broken nib~~
> ~~of memory, there'll be~~

> ~~no more signatures~~
> ~~with this pen.~~

What it means to ask
what it means

is what it means
to ask

what it means. Thought,
a wind

that disturbs pooled days;
all facts

are disputed,
their position

is unfixed, liable to change
of color, status,

attachment to belief.
I'm destitute

of spontaneity, yielding
to the will of others

the fact
of having lived,

tumbling into a crack
of memory, like a key

dropped in confusion
through a grate.

~~If it gleams,~~
~~you can be sure~~

~~it wasn't lost that long ago.~~
~~Gleaming or dull,~~

~~it's scarcely worth~~
~~the effort of being found~~

Dementia

If you hang out long enough in the nursing home,
  someone will eventually offer you dessert...

The mind? An architecture
in which levels
cannot
sufficiently
differentiate
stories

a dwindled source
of will
to live

Swell

to apart

at the seams

The tea

is a golden pool

cooling in stillness

like a man in bed all day and night

Prayers fall from his lip—

they never seem to rise.

Square of sun

crossed by shadow—

gift of a window

set at his feet.

Like a face,
the days
are entirely outward. Their will

retreats
into
involuntary
functions

pleasures

contentments

impediments

What limits can we set to implication?

What is your mother's maiden name?

What city were you born in?

What is the name of your dog?

DEEP TIME

Failure to connect
one worry with its opposite
left me unbalanced.

Tomorrow is a cloud
that bursts,
we take shelter in each other.

~~A hole~~
~~in the grind~~
~~where the granules fall~~[+]

> [+]~~But before they fall~~
> ~~they are solid,~~
> ~~won't fit the opening.~~

Thread of logic
stripped in the turn
of a clock,

gnarl and scab
of a tree: my eyes
were leaky

and I sank
in sleep, dreamt of sea,
woke up tired from treading water.

~~Water collects around my feet~~
~~and seeps~~
~~where I can't go,~~

~~a whole~~
~~in the ground~~
~~where the graveless call.~~

~~I cross the brook~~
~~so shallow~~
~~only my sole gets wet~~

~~I....~~

Nothing metaphysical about it:
we're of the earth, on it.
Our ethical grounds

are what dirty our hands.
Short enough to be crossed, vast enough to get lost
in: time[2]

    [2] ~~will continue,~~
     ~~whether it drags us~~
     ~~along or not.~~

is what skips the instant
it holds in un-
skippable sequence.

My Scabies Year

The soft outer covering

of vertebrates

vibrates

when thousands

bore through

in hard purpose,

a living serration

cut through

sensation

uncleanly.

My skin's alive

and scratches loudly.

~~A scraping~~

~~taken~~

~~for testing~~

~~continues to die~~

~~apart from its host.~~

With fingernails

exacerbating

circumstances

notwithstanding

any heightened sense

of pleasure

radiates infection.

The itching is terrible.

Heat makes it worse.

~~Yet I can stand~~

~~in a hot shower~~

~~thirty minutes, the sensation~~

~~exquisite.~~

Infinitesimal

fecal

matter

glows in

the scab

all skin becomes

after scratching.

~~Those parts of us~~

~~we cannot occupy~~

~~or know, where~~

~~others have trod.~~

~~My mind~~

~~is a blank~~

~~rage~~

~~that fills with any~~

~~capable noise.~~

The master

of a sense

perception,

a clutch of

darkness.

~~Scrubbing,~~

~~I am the brush~~

~~filled with the~~

~~grit of any skin~~

~~I touch.~~

Like a dog

who races

into waves

and yaps,

racing back

when the waves defy him, I dance

into time

and scream,

but there is no dancing back.

HERE'S THAT RAINY DAY

A functional
incapacity to think
even a second ahead of my own
actions, even when the second is past,
receding far
into the fog of never was.

~~I forgot the emotion~~

~~attached to those shapes,~~

~~only the colors~~

~~remain~~

~~in place of a story.~~

posteriority

is a form
whose content

            is to be
the days

don't run on time
      because there is
   no schedule free enough
to fill
            ~~fairy circles~~
~~winding down~~

               ~~& so~~

         ~~life became the illustration~~

      ~~of a principle by which~~

      ~~I act on impulse,~~

               ~~understanding nothing~~

      Here's that

rainy day

~~insulated, I conduct~~

~~insulation~~
  ~~for the wire~~
   ~~that conducts~~
       ~~tradition across~~
           ~~a flammable expanse~~

Time

softens and collapses

like an apple in a pot

over heat

a river,
seed,
lamp,
wind,
cloud,

a colony collapse

~~not equal to anything that is equal~~

~~the merit has not decayed~~

The pea under the mattress
that keeps me awake

is the name I can't remember,
the face I can't place.

FERMENT

"to create delicacies rather than decomposition"
    (Sandor Katz)

Like the fuzz
on a yellow quince,
society is rubbed away,

like sleep
in the ripening
of a dream

Because the state
is magnanimous
and wide

bruised pear

Daylight Savings Time

~~boiled-down grape must~~
~~dried fruits~~

~~my protection is out of date~~

A resource follows elevation away
from the highest point.
As if time

were a writing desk
upon which life
transpired

with something akin
to penmanship
The sawed-off ends

of trees
in back of a truck
called Tundra.

~~Paring away what doesn't~~
~~matter leaves nothing~~
~~that stands on its own~~

A blur of color
veined with branches
A giant frayed leaf of yellowish green

Birds
are augurs
of color

if nothing else. Love
is a razer
that leaves stubble,

a consequence
one learns best
by feel.

Late Afternoon in Winter, Eyes Drooping

No more words are all I have,
just a book
open on my lap.

~~Bias of the day~~
~~that turns a face away,~~
~~darkened.~~

~~My posture,~~
~~contorted~~
~~as an ampersand,~~

~~joining one moment~~
~~and another,~~
~~but I'm not there~~

A self-

censored

datum

smiling on sleep,

I run

on and on

in sleep's

opposite direction, seeking all that might

obstruct

my forward progress.

~~"I"~~

~~is a diphthong—~~

~~sliding, made whole~~

~~in the glide of enunciation.~~

Intimacy and estrangement, different shadings of a color,

modulated by temperature You're smart

to the touch, I said,

and when sensation

traveled through the system, maintaining contact from afar,

I leapt

at a chance

that couldn't bear

my weight

Like a sigh's undertaking,

verbose to the end,

a forgotten cigarette

that leaves its ash

suspended, a burn mark on the world

~~Like the silver of a moon~~

~~sliding off the water~~

~~into darkness, myself~~

~~on the other side~~

~~Like the spine of a book~~

~~whose riffling pages~~

~~stir the night~~

Turn the volume all the way down, and lower still,

even the silence is way too loud.

A Period of Mourning

~~Let each year swallow~~

~~itself and be the purge~~

~~of undigested~~

~~nourishment.~~ The hills of snow

contract, become heavy

If I walk across the trees'

shadows, and look up,

the sky is blinding,

The icy driveway turns to slush

and I slip

as I walk

to the back door.

~~The torn-out gas station,~~

~~its tanks pulled up and the holes filled in,~~

~~the cellophane crinkle~~

~~of partially frozen puddles,~~

~~a soft sweater~~

~~that slips to the floor:~~

~~give me time,~~

~~I will name everything that's past.~~

                                        Reasoning

cuts through
a multitude

of sensations. ~~Perplexity~~

is a mode of apprehension

neither here nor there. Numbness
takes

a feeling form. Like putting
on a coat

that's upside down,

searching for an arm

that isn't there. All voices

come together

to be noise. The still air

tortured into movement

by a song. Time

opens a box
that space closes. The day

~~has a winter look. Not cold,~~
~~but bare; rubbed raw~~

~~by earth's rotation.~~
~~I part the universe~~

~~with every step,~~
~~it heals itself~~

~~as instantly~~
                    ~~Tasked~~

~~with holding down~~
~~the night with sleep~~
                    ~~the day~~

~~blew a gust~~
~~of emptiness~~

~~in my direction~~
~~Intentions matter,~~

~~and like all matter~~
~~decay~~

All my thoughts

are ajar,
        but my heart

is closed,
        a screen door banging in wind,

the wooden door sealed to.

HOSPICE

Fatigue
is a chronic inflammation
of the edge

of grief
goes sick,
unauthorized

and steering clear of care ~~Personhood~~
~~takes control~~
~~of the matter~~

~~it disturbs,~~
~~pulling us down~~
~~into a hole~~

~~its weight makes~~ Pressure
forms a shape
propped

into an opening
smaller than its disclosure.
And this is what we consider death,

a budding. Grief
is the opposite,
weakening

a structure, allowing emotion
to collapse ~~To spill~~
~~milk~~

~~yet drink it~~
~~comes to grief~~
~~goes sour, curdled, surpassing~~

~~expiration date~~
To express
an emotion

in propositional language:
"it feels really bad."
OK, but is there another way?

~~Dimensions that can't~~
~~be measured~~
~~with a ruler Less~~

~~than the sum~~
~~of her parts, which occupy~~
~~her every waking moment~~

My posture sensed
there was trouble[‡]

    [‡]~~Before the Law~~
    ~~Outside a Door~~

    ~~In the time it took my foot~~
    ~~to fall asleep~~
    ~~a setting sun foretold~~

    ~~the end of the world~~
    ~~as we know it,~~
    ~~and took off~~

    ~~for safety—~~
    ~~but I couldn't follow;~~
    ~~my foot had fallen asleep.~~

before I could tell

my muscles to ease.
Alone,
the rain is silent.

But all it strikes
comes alive with sound
bearing down in thought.

~~Mom,~~
~~dad,~~
~~I'll see you~~
~~in a while,~~

~~looking different~~
~~I imagine.~~

~~But you~~

~~will know~~

~~it's me~~

~~by this~~

~~phrase:~~

FUNERAL

A meaning so full it can only be lifted when a little is poured off.

To sleep, perchance to grieve.

The way one fumbles with an unfamiliar lock,
switching between the keys. The way one feels
with an unfamiliar key, seeking a proper fit.

Putting a little pressure on the teeth.

Tongue of metal, a smile of bone.

What calls them back is not their name,
or anything we want of them
In fact, they don't come back.

Out of the freshly laundered
pockets of time

came a wad of paper bearing
irretrievable information.[‡]

  [‡] ~~The piece of paper~~
   ~~slipped from my grasp, and grasping~~

   ~~slipped from consciousness;~~
   ~~and it all continued within me, dead to the world[a]~~

    [a] ~~A steep path~~
     ~~where every step~~

     ~~met with a root~~
     ~~that maddened the feet.~~

I call this waking up.

My Countenance

Curve of mouth, bound between
what didn't get said
and never got thought: horizon I'd reach

and can't even see—
except in this photo:
a sadness that strangers mistake

for listening, that has no tension
in its line
of inquiry...unlike that other

pounded from metal
and bent into shape, held in place
until the muscles ache.

If I had a smile
for this occasion
it would be

a painted grin rolling down the runway,
armed to the teeth, bound by mission

above the clouds.

The piles of snow sink into themselves

My features

supplant the order: smile

OUT OF TWIG

OK, now spread
   your hands

wide, take in the world.
    It's not yours.

~~Pull the wind out of your hair,~~
~~let it go to the high branches.~~

~~Their tips yield way to a breeze,~~
~~the roots hold fast~~

     ~~Felt~~
     Felled

~~by~~ like a tree
that cut the wind, caught

~~my ear~~

my eye

with the shimmer of movement
that went nowhere,
sending sound everywhere...

When the wind rises
there's a clatter
of hardened rain
against the glass

Something moves,
plotted
in a graph
of cries by birds who keep
their distance

~~Pissing away from the empty trail,~~
~~listening for voices~~

~~colors rarify the light~~

life's ~~but a dream not yet~~ forgotten

~~Scrambled infinity~~

The hum of a truck-
bed rising by a tree,
lifting up a man
to prune a limb.

~~Posture is the collision~~
~~of nature and culture.~~

~~I stand on this~~
~~principle, which~~

~~weighs on my shoulders.~~

All my leaves communicating,
twisting but not free
from a wooden
understanding
flexible and strong.

REFLECTION IN A PASSING GLASS

Since it is not myself I see, but a synecdoche,

my body (it speeds along—
it spurns—it yields), what wonder

I feel the world rush into my mind
although it's my mind rushing into the world.

I vanish
into myself, putting forward
an imposter
on my behalf.

A snarl—a grimace—

a scowl—sneer—glare. ~~Only time~~
~~and its widening trap~~

                    Regret
cuts into the past
with deliberate strokes,
though each cut piece

adheres
to the one before.

A present-tense mobility
slipping
from awareness
into thinking

Their border has no guard,
only elevation keeps
a wanderer
from going back.

~~The tops of the trees are agitated~~
~~but the clouds above them drift serene~~

CALUMNY

The truth? It's as plain as the tongue in my mouth,
which holds still
and suffers on. [1]

[1] Crossing a threshold
  of anger, it stirs. Anger
  giving way to anger

  where the anger touches anger
  and pulls back, a tide
  that eventually returns.

My tongue, a soft arc
of metal with a hard
crease: I cut through all purpose

with it silent, leaving
a little wake of whispers
in my head.

A swell to rock
a placid face, it comes ashore
with minor splash, sets down a lace-

like trace of froth,[2]

[2] and seep, and spittle,

twaddle,
muddle,[3]

[3] anger, anger, anger

DEPRESSION

In sleep
the informal
concept of comfort
is a blanket's weight
~~spread across the sun,~~

~~sun shrunk to the size of my bed~~
yet it shrouds all form.
I dream,

and run

with feet nailed to the floor
before

~~the dam breaks~~ the night slips

into wrinkled metaphors
that refuse to flatten.

Why is this naught
different from all other

you say
the colors
fade—I say they linger

~~Chronology~~

~~conquers all,~~

~~surmounts~~

~~the matter~~

~~ticked off~~

~~its list~~

~~piece by piece~~

~~The future~~

~~is an escape route,~~

eventually a dead end

And yet the past

never catches up

The foot
fallen asleep

has the heaviness
of philosophy,

but I can stand on that
ponderous weight

It's only painful
when I try to walk

I'll take a sip

from your same

stream, twice

I'll carry away

my trash

when I am done

Stretching a lie

to make ends meet:

I'll *no* you with my eyes

though my mouth yields a grudging *yes.*

Testamentary Device

Shreds tipped with gray
like a moth's wing
fill the transparent globe
below the blade.

~~They spill~~

~~from an evening~~

~~or two~~

~~of unperformed restraint.~~

The nubby branches
of a dying tree,
contorted, black
against the white.

~~What's left to say. What remains unsaid.~~

No dreaming, just wandering, all night long.
A voice that gives me away. Sometimes

I wish I could fold up
my life
in an envelope,

put it in a book,
the book in a box,
the box in an attic.

      Who lives downstairs?
Is it me?
        I mark the mortal

increments of time
with all my extended length,

bearing down
with feeling
on a feeling
out of reach
of pencil underhand.

MIRROR

Looking at you I take my stand
on ground that answers back.

~~Stubborn surface~~

   ~~of a shrug~~

      ~~that slides away from what would stand~~

      ~~still, certain of where it is,~~

      ~~but going nowhere.~~

~~The twin of speciousness~~ Chime,

as day stirs
a trickle, little sound,
into the stream of all
I hear:

~~weighed down by the dark,~~
        ~~which has no substance to think of~~

a thawing,

rising,

accelerating,

thunderous

dream

~~It seeps~~
~~from a sponge of light,~~

~~it sits in a bucket of rain,~~
~~the day~~

It gets away
without volition

Withdraws me
from this moment

to think ~~The yard~~
~~keeps pace~~

~~with the spinning world~~
~~on which it is set.~~ Muddling through,
but not all the way

~~making space~~
~~for the unremembered,~~

~~which never goes away.~~ Wakefulness
helps the colors

brighten, the edges sharpen. Thought
snags there, rips. ~~Muscle and fat~~

~~shape me from within, the posture~~
~~an expression~~

~~of how I feel about it.~~
~~My face is scarcely~~

~~relevant—it belongs~~
~~to the others. And yet~~[1]

[1] **The Soul Is Dark**

The mirror in which
I look into my own

eyes keeps me
at arm's length.

When the light
goes out

there is nothing more
to be seen, yet I am there.

Until-When-Grasses

Why does time
have a single
direction? It flows

without end, falls short,
goes out. Among trees
it signifies

the firm
and the gnarled.
A fog's height

unsettled
underfoot
around peaks. In the spring,

roads swell and crack;
in summer,
they're repaired.

With autumn comes tar,
shining black.
With winter: ice and salt.

What comes after
the afterlife
has been discarded

as an answer
to grief
is grief

without question. Time
out of sequence
of question and answer.

Sunlight creates
but can't grasp
the shadow

of feral trees. Clocks chatter,
time is silent—
not quite a conversation.

Yahrzeit

There is nothing but Shadow and Vapour in the Thing.
   (Defoe)

I miss that head.[‡]

> [‡] ~~A mind that tightens~~
> ~~the bolt, a mind that loosens.~~
> ~~A mind that [   ]~~
> ~~[   ], a mind that [   ].~~

A weight on the pillow,

eyes closed,

seeing nothing

reportable any more.

~~The spirit~~
~~is a noxious~~
~~gas.~~ The skin

is an organ
of perception
that can fail us

we

frail in it

then spirit away.

~~Combustibility dissipates~~

~~A severed connection between now and then~~

But to step
on that head?
Cross over
a border

of grief
to its
other
side?

Like a kitten,
always restless;
a fly, ever
in search
of unclean things;
a fire,
never satisfied

~~you in your calendar~~
~~box, waiting for the~~
~~bottom to drop out~~

The rain,
arrogant in dismissal
of the cloud
emptied out,

lofty in regard
for the ground
in which it sinks,
sinks.

Ghostly Spring

The five stages of history Isolation Barter

Amnesia

Denial Anger Depression

Everything gets to happen
at least once, hypothetically;
the eventual *will* occur.
It all comes down

like snow, but doesn't stick My heart

is a cup that never fills.

I sip from it on occasion.

I'm lost,
I'm not found.

I was lost
but now

I'm not
found, only accommodated.

Forecast:
past due,

and gone to seed,
from there to wind,

ground,

stalk,

leaf

The forsythia is exuberant,
alive with yellow

when all the other plants feign dead.
Yellow is the apparition of my April, ghostly spring

CARE

I take interest
in what depletes interest
and give myself in the bargain.

Will solidifies chaos
and chaos disintegrates will

~~To take up a particle of~~
~~dust and build a shrine~~

~~I stop listening~~
~~and wish I could stop hearing~~

~~The minutes ding~~
~~and dong~~
~~the day~~

~~How does it follow~~
~~from what~~
~~comes next?~~

Leaves lift
from trees
in full,
let colors fall

~~Pain~~
~~is not communicated~~
~~but illustrated,~~
~~an afterthought~~
~~not given to words~~

~~Down is not a direction but state of mind~~

Coping isn't a mechanism, but a saw. Its teeth

a chip

of paint

knocked off

my wall

As when a fly
slips inside
a partly
open door

Spooled out
like a ribbon
of oil
from a ship

A slippery slope?

The slope itself

slid down

and all that was left

—commensal bacteria.

The spoils
of duty
come to grief

so suddenly, one feels more
surprise
than sadness

When light returns

the world to me

I recognize the source

of all familiarity

remains the dark,

myself.

At Sea Level

Reaching
with words
for what sense
cannot obtain. ~~I feel~~
~~my way~~
~~in flip~~
~~flops over~~
~~gravel.~~ Memory,
a flat surface
stretched by current. What little
I've learned
floats away
on all I've forgotten.
~~Boredom~~
~~sparks~~
~~disinterest,~~
~~which burns~~
~~all it touches~~

Two petals, motionless
in the sand
of a parking lot:

half a yellow flower—
no, an old butterfly. ~~Color~~

~~is a form of solar power.~~ Stubble

of growth in arid ground.

It is enough, almost,

that the sea stops short of my feet.

Houses at the edge of the marsh

like broken teeth
in a lower jaw

Birds circle

the comprehending sky

The tide retreats

yet waves keep coming

The horizon

is a massive hole
that springs
no leak.

BENJAMIN FRIEDLANDER is a poet, scholar, and editor. His poetry collections include *A Knot Is Not a Tangle* (Krupskaya, 2000), *The Missing Occasion of Saying Yes* (Subpress, 2007), *Citizen Cain* (Salt, 2011), and *One Hundred Etudes* (Edge, 2012). Currently, he teaches American literature and poetics at the University of Maine, where he edits the scholarly journal *Paideuma*.

www.ingramcontent.com/pod-product-compliance
Lightning Source LLC
Chambersburg PA
CBHW031447120626
46545CB00006B/2587